I AM a REBEL GIRL

I AM a REBEL GiRL
a JOURNAL TO START REVOLUTIONS

FRANCESCA CAVALLO
ELENA FAVILLI

TiMBUKTU

I Am a Rebel Girl, *Good Night Stories for Rebel Girls*, and *Good Night Stories for Rebel Girls 2* are available at special quantity discounts for bulk purchase for sale promotions, premiums, fundraising, and educational needs. For details, write to wholesale@rebelgirls.co

Created by Francesca Cavallo and Elena Favilli
Art Direction by Giulia Flamini
Graphic Design by Annalisa Ventura
Illustrations by Martina Paukova, Kate Prior, and Camila Rosa
Cover Design by Kate Prior

Printed in Canada

The paper used to print this book is made from wood grown in well-managed forests. The manufacturing processes conform to the environmental regulations of the country of origin.

www.rebelgirls.co
ISBN: 978-0-9978958-4-1

First Edition
10 9 8 7 6 5 4 3 2 1

**Freedom
is the destination,**

**And the map
is yours to draw.**

Contents

★ Introduction ★

Dearest Rebel,

Growing up as little girls, we've been taught to color within the lines that other people have drawn for us. We've been taught to say "yes" even when we wanted to say "no." We've been taught to take up as little space as we could.

It's time to stop passing these lessons on.

With this journal, we give you a mirror to explore your identity without fear. We can reach equality only if we stop frantically selecting the few parts of ourselves that are acceptable to society and embrace the fact that we have the right to be whole.

This is the place where you can celebrate your ambition without reserve, love your body without shame, organize rallies, plan businesses, and work out the details of your adventurous life.

So, if the world tells you to shrink, we'll ask you to visualize yourself as a giant. If the world tells you to be quiet, we'll pass you a megaphone! If the world questions women's rights, we'll give you space to write your own bill of rights.

I Am a Rebel Girl is designed to help you train your rebel spirit, embrace your potential with joy and determination, and be an agent of change.

The Good Night Stories for Rebel Girls series is about the daring deeds of many great women. *I Am a Rebel Girl* is about you, your story, and your revolution.

When you hold this journal, know that you are not alone. Sitting at many other desks and kitchen tables, or hunched over their legs on a train or on a bus, there are many other girls and women who, just like you, are dreaming, drawing, and building a different world.

We can't wait to see what you will accomplish!

Yours,
Francesca Cavallo
Elena Favilli

This is how I see myself.

because I'm
playful

I have the right to . . .

Own a house

Have a pet

Ride a bike

17

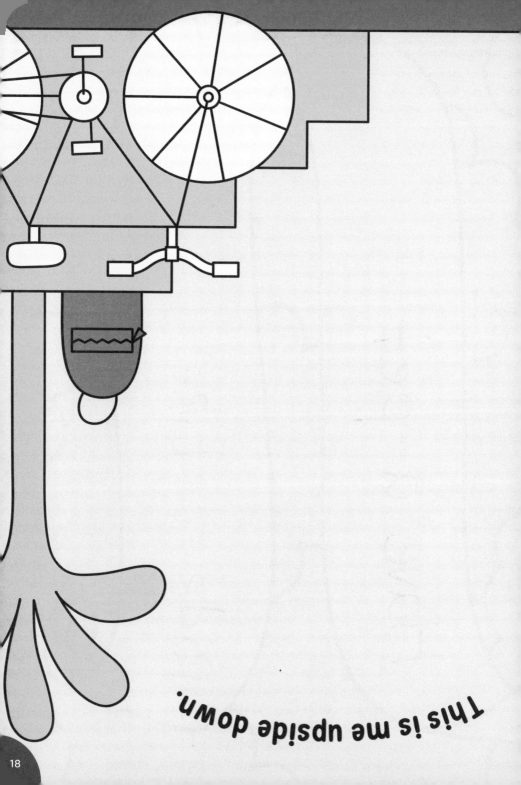

This is me upside down.

My everyday look

I AM
POWERFUL!

My family

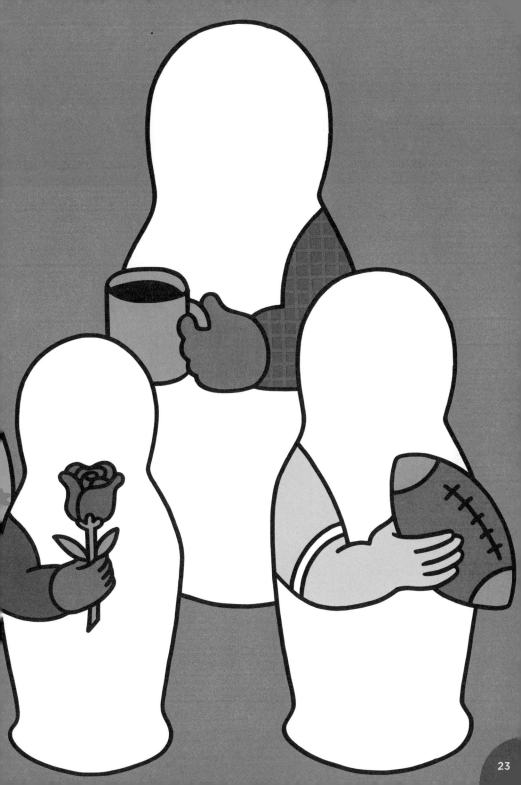

Here's what my family thinks of me . . .

This is how I sit.

This is how I sleep.

Love notes to my favorite body parts

Dear Stomach, Thanks for filling me up so I'm not hungry

Dear Brain, Thanks for helping me think and helping me with my emotions

Dear Spine,
thank you for
letting me
do bridges
in acro, I'm
getting
pretty
flexible

Dear Hands,
Thanks for
letting me
lift up
things
when
needed

Foods that cheer me up

pasta
Ice cream
cake/carrot cake
whipped cream
pancakes
chocolate

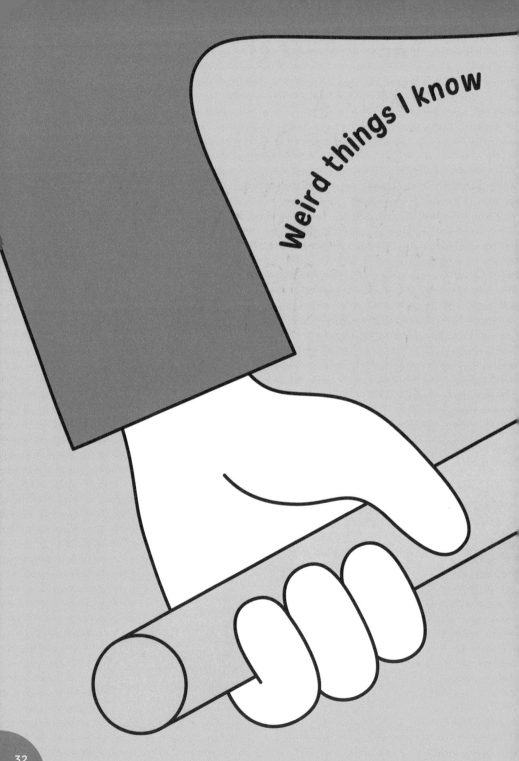

Weird things I know

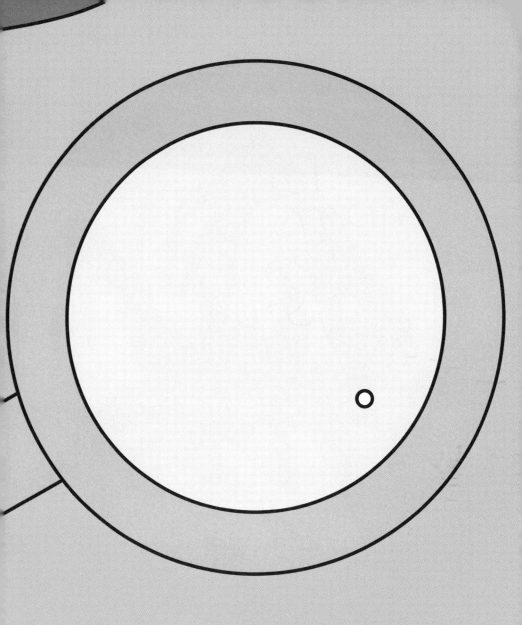

Fears I have

Fears I don't have

Things I say

Getting pajamas on

Ice cream

Hanging out with my family

Going to the movies

Going
shopping

Going to a
pet store

to

eating

1.

2.

3.

4.

5.

Rebel
Girls'

Playlist

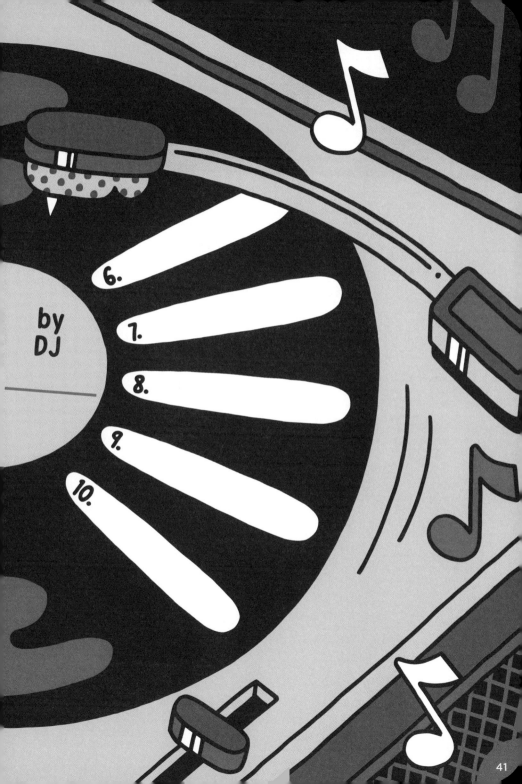

by
DJ

6.

7.

8.

9.

10.

Animals
who really get me

Things I can lift!

A ton
of books

My brother

A tissue
box

Me belly up

My signature dance move

Things I think about when the lights go out

Words I love

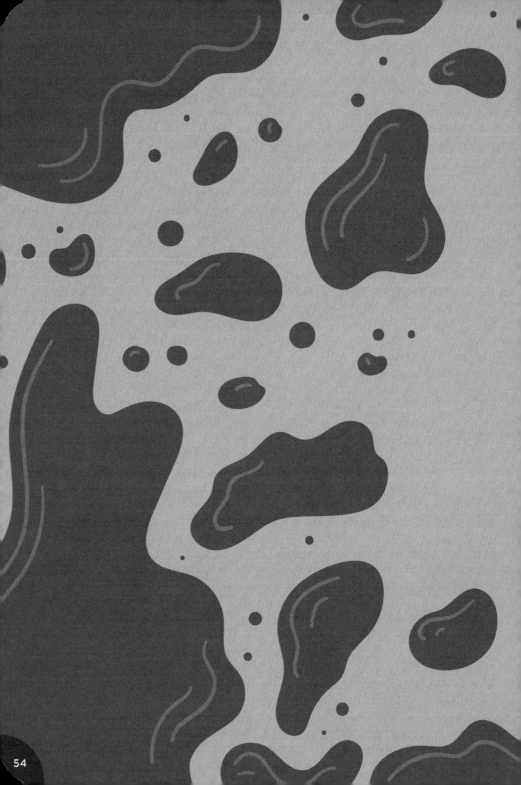

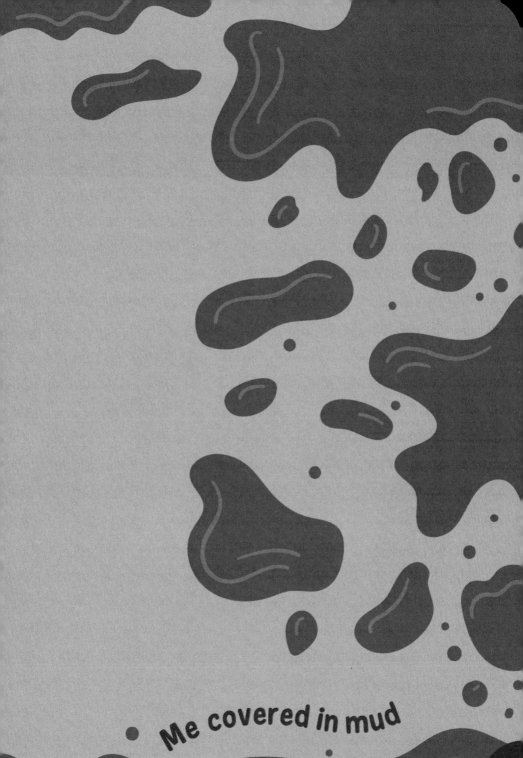

Me covered in mud

Stuff I broke

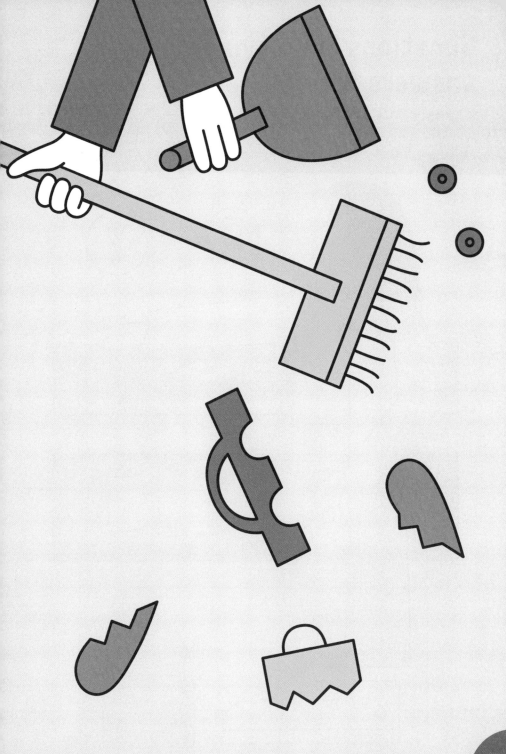

Questions I don't have answers for

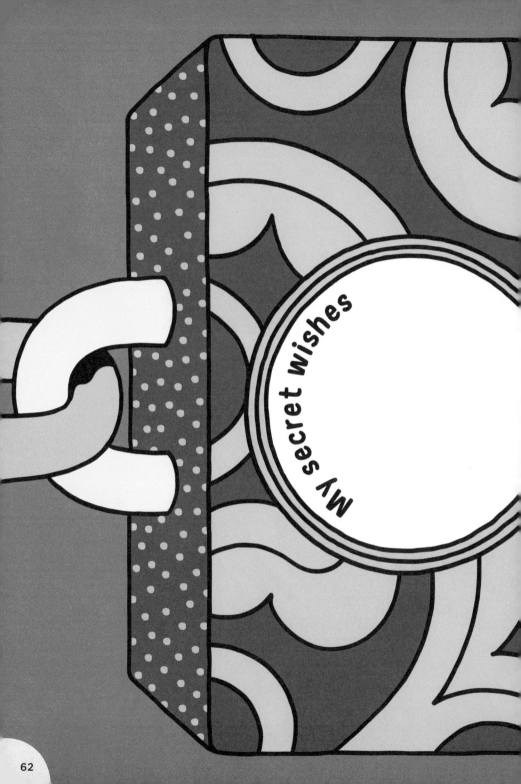

My secret wishes

Glue these pages together to keep your secret.

Things I want
IN my closet

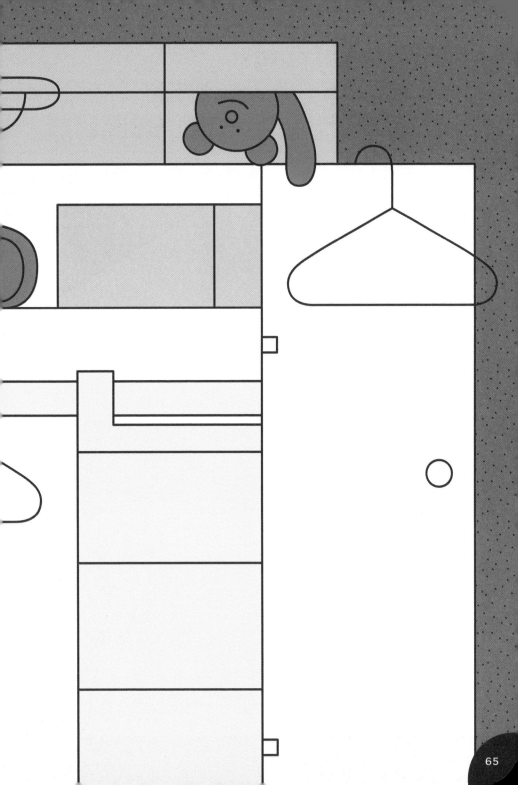

Things
I want OUT
of my closet

Important words I invented

People I want to meet

THE TINY MARTIAN

HOW DID YOU GET HERE?

Secret code

A	Z	J	Q	S	H
B	Y	K	P	T	G
C	X	L	O	U	F
D	W	M	N	V	E
E	V	N	M	W	D
F	U	O	L	X	C
G	T	P	K	Y	B
H	S	Q	J	Z	A
I	R	R	~~I~~		

Secret message

Secret code

A _____   H _____   O _____   V _____

B _____   I _____   P _____   W _____

C _____   J _____   Q _____   X _____

D _____   K _____   R _____   Y _____

E _____   L _____   S _____   Z _____

F _____   M _____   T _____

G _____   N _____   U _____

IT'S OK
TO BE
AFRAID.

Stuff that
makes me angry

Villains I'm going to defeat

Thanos!
(Marvel/Avengers)

← Loki
(same thing)

Red
skull

Robbers

Pet
thiefs

ZOOM
(same
thing)

The man
in yellow
(Flash)

Things worth fighting for

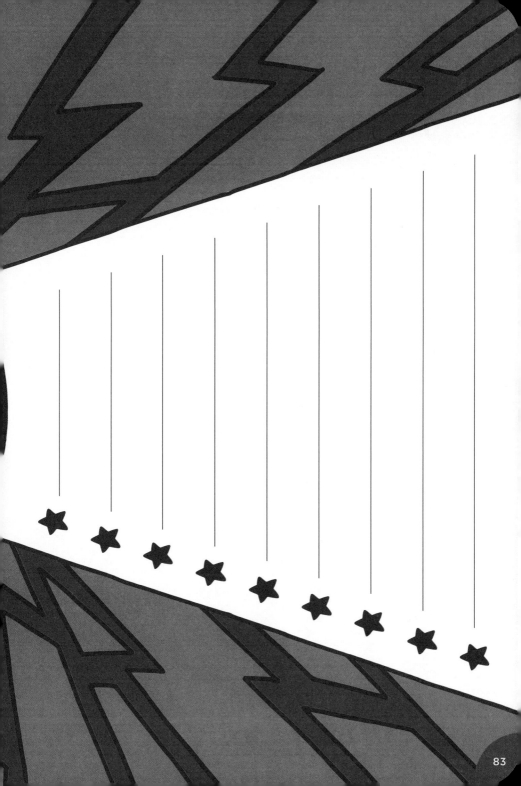

INTERVIEW WITH
THE BRAVEST WOMAN I KNOW

....

THE PIRATE QUEEN

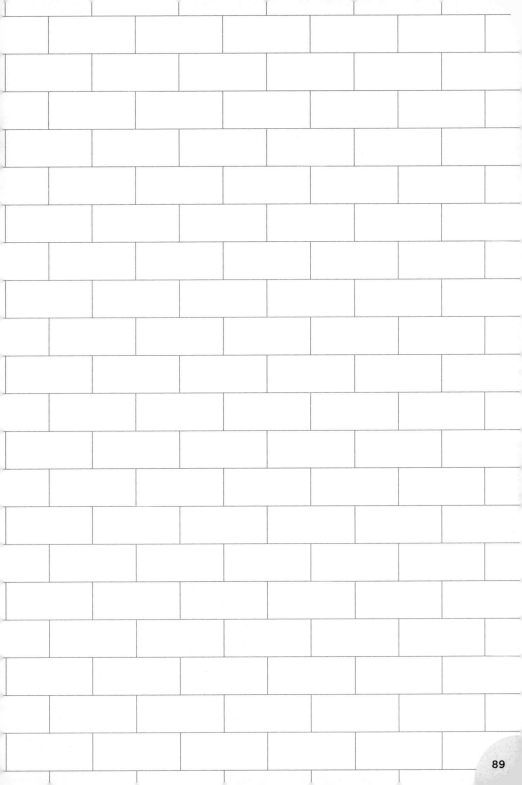

These rules don't make sense to me.

My march

Dear future me,

I wanted to tell you that the time I'm writing this, the corona virus is going on. It sucks! Also, this is the time were looking into getting a dog. I still have a fear of Red skull. Also, in about 3 months from now I'll be moving to Minnisota. Please write me

back and tell me
if you like the house
there. Also tell me
what the dog is
called and if it's a
boy or girl.
(I hope girl).

P.S. This was the
day we made a
bunny trap!
Past you,
-Isabelle

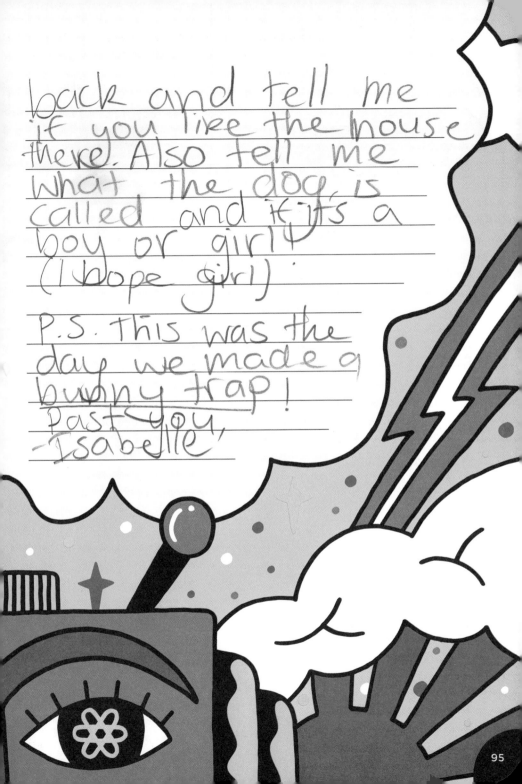

95

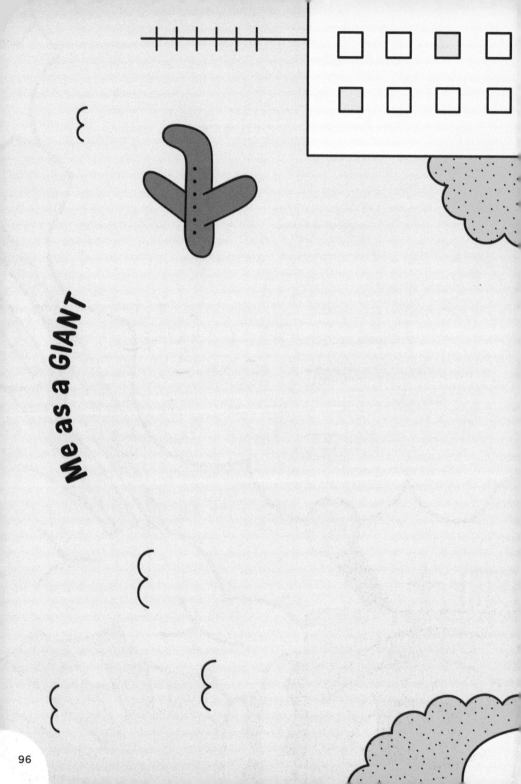

Me as a GIANT

An incredible invention

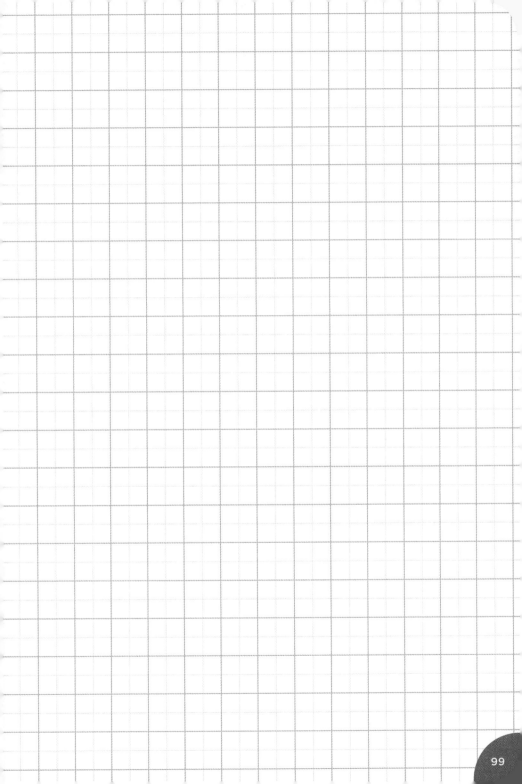

Things my friends are good at

My business

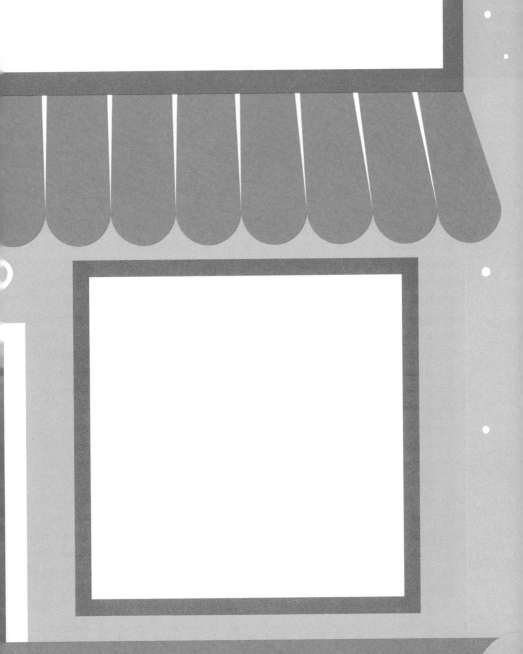

Ways to make $10

Ways to save $10

Something weird happened to me . . .

Books I'm going to write

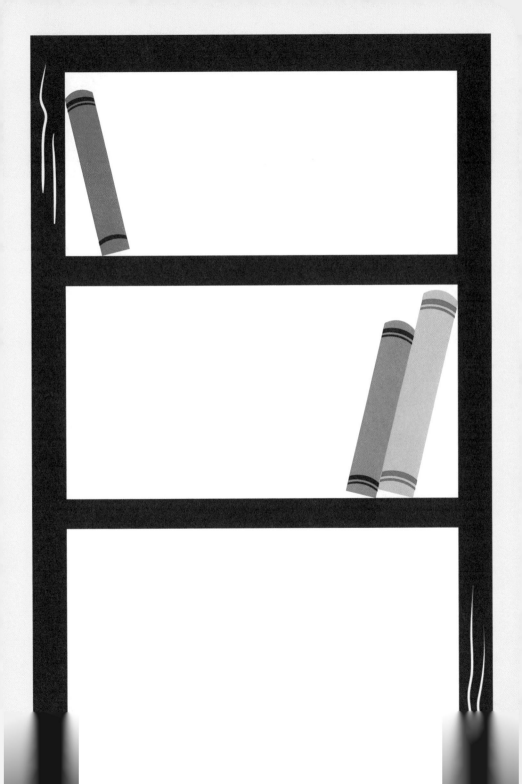

Me as a fairy

112

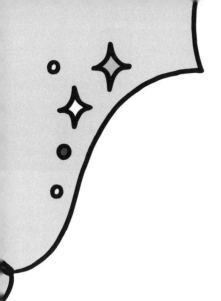

My career plan

Age 18

Age 90

Age 60

Age 40

Age 25

Dear _____ ,

I need help with . . .

_____
_____
_____
_____
_____
_____
_____
_____
_____
_____
_____
_____
_____
_____

Would you help me?

☐   ☐   ☐

Yes   **No**   _____

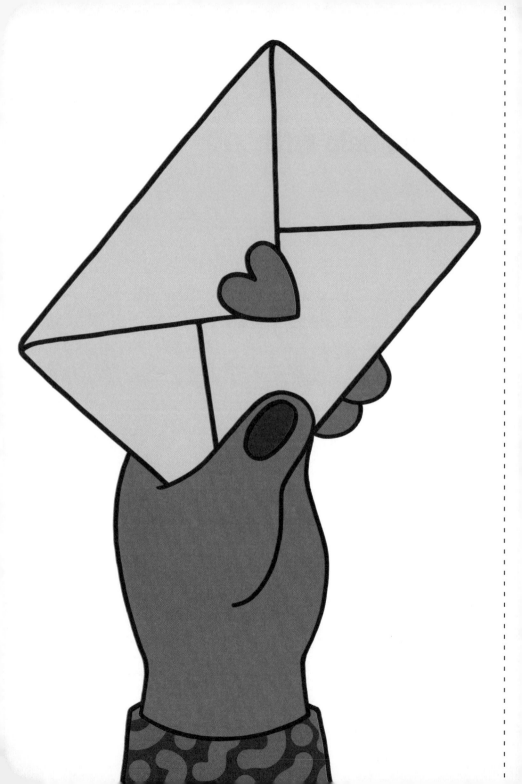

I'M THE
RIGHT PERSON
AT THE RIGHT TIME
IN THE RIGHT
PLACE.

This award
goes to . . . ME!

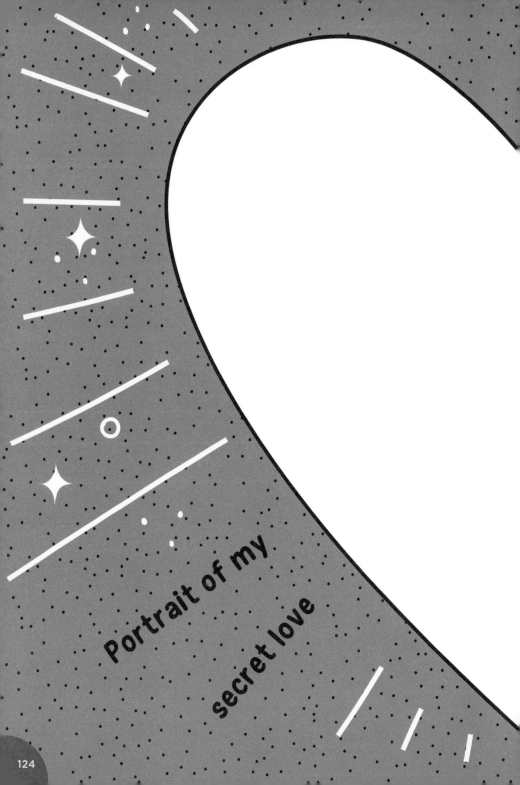

Portrait of my
secret love

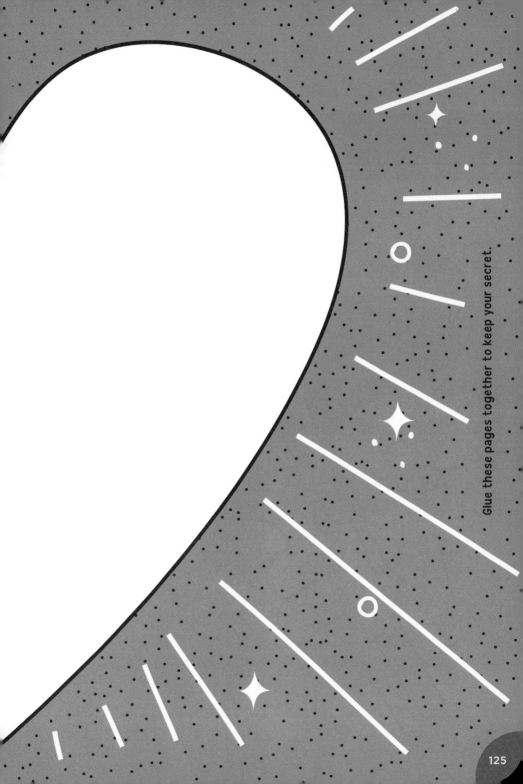

Glue these pages together to keep your secret.

WILL YOU GO OUT WITH ME?

When:
6:00

Where:
Pizzaria

Oh, yes!   Not sure   No!

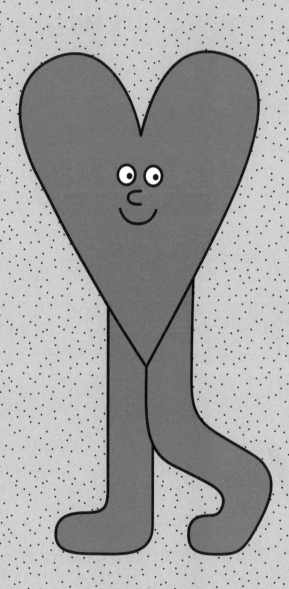

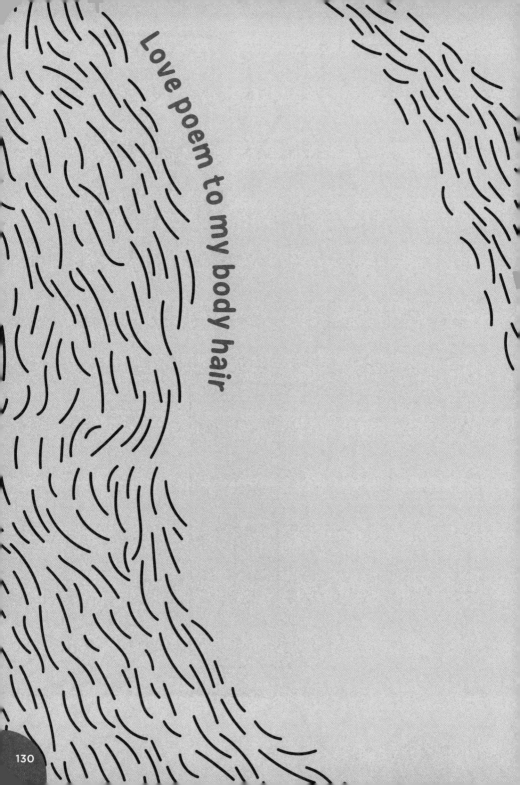

Love poem to my body hair

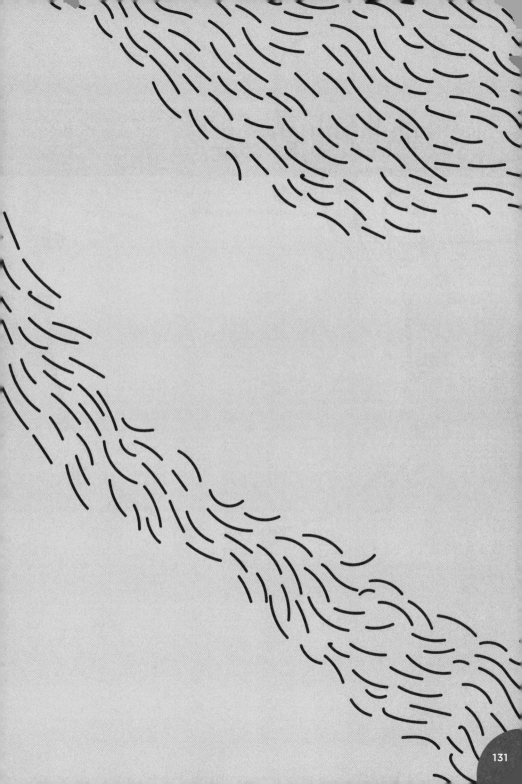

Feelings I hide behind

my sunglasses

Rebel Girls' Fort

Rebel girls
I'm proud of

Rebel Girls' Rap ♥

_____

_____

_____

_____

_____

_____

_____

_____

_____

_____

_____

A serenade to my love

Important words
in other languages

Plan for a day of adventure

Me on a mountain

Books to bring on a desert island

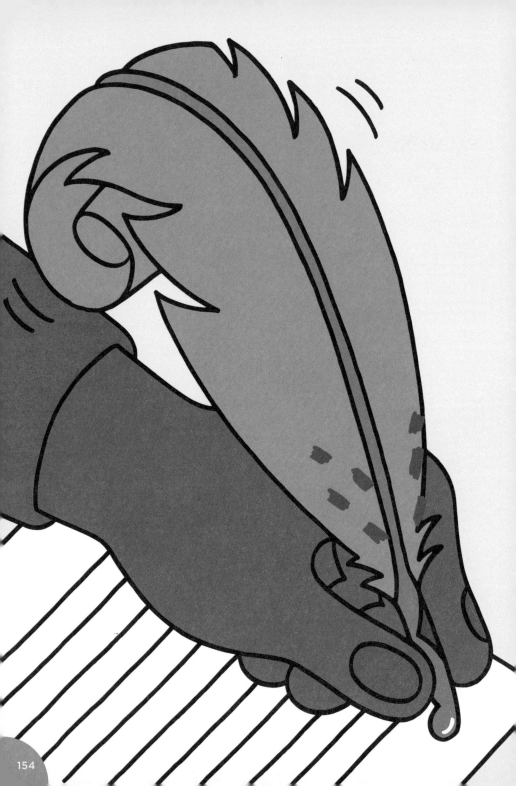

Dear _____ ,

I miss you . . .

_____
_____
_____
_____
_____
_____
_____
_____
_____
_____
_____
_____
_____
_____
_____
_____
_____

I'M
WORTH
IT!

Questions
I haven't been asked

BEFORE

AFTER

MADAM PRESIDENT

My currency

Things I'm thirsty for

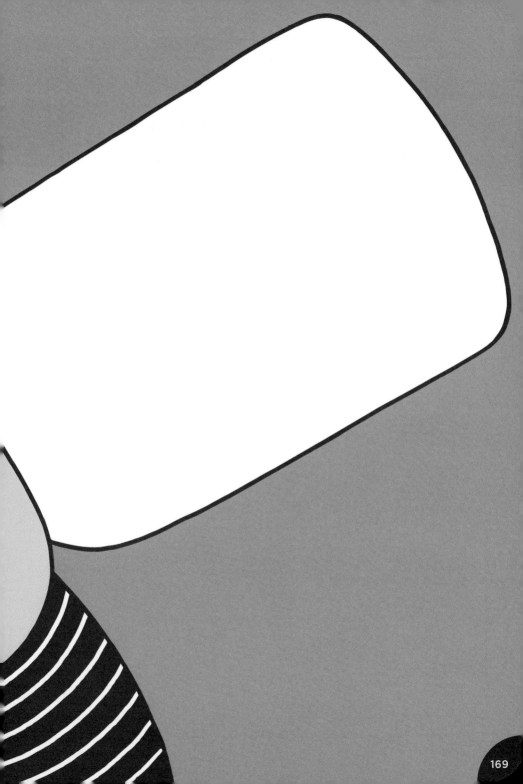

CUP _of monkeys_

CUP _____

CUP _____

CUP _____

SPOON _of lions_

SPOON _____

Recipe for disaster

The Sadness Corner

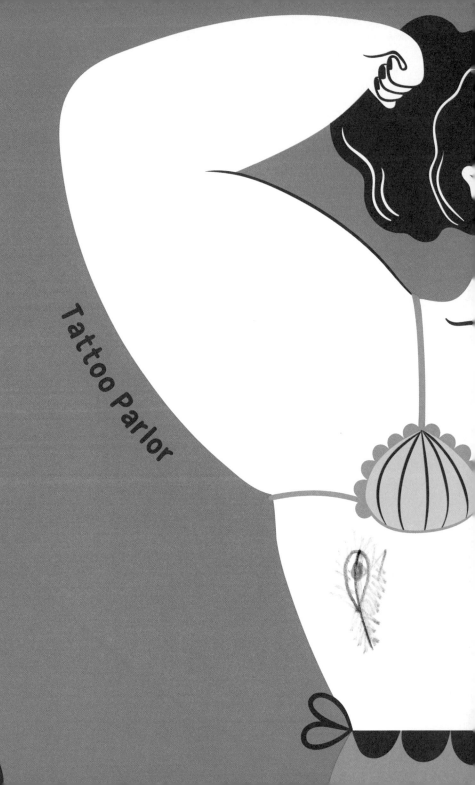

Tattoo Parlor

Letter to
an elected
representative

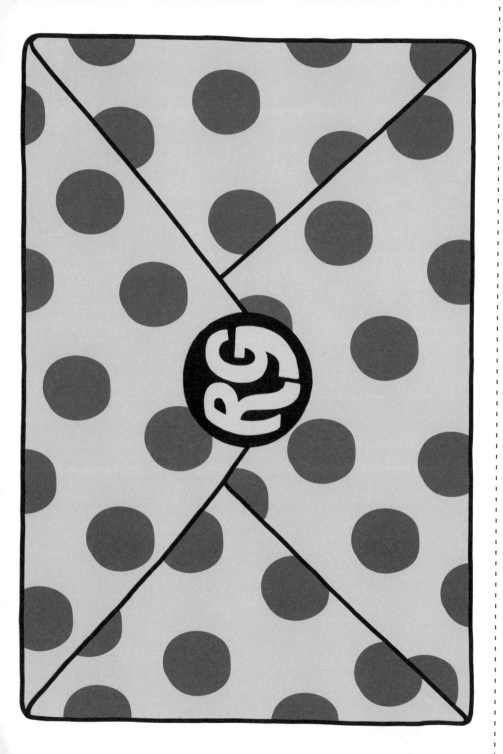

THE REVOLUTION STARTS WITH ME!

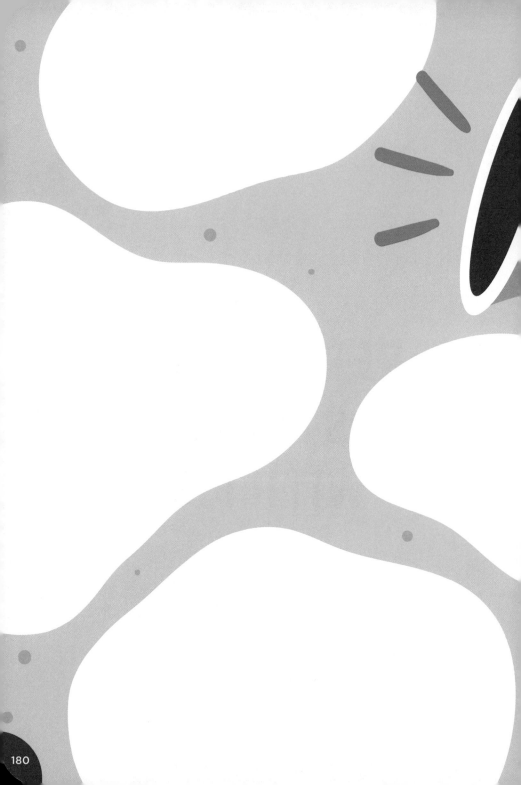

Mind-blowing ideas

Me underwater

What my friends
think of me ...

Sell this page!

I sold this
page for

Things to let go

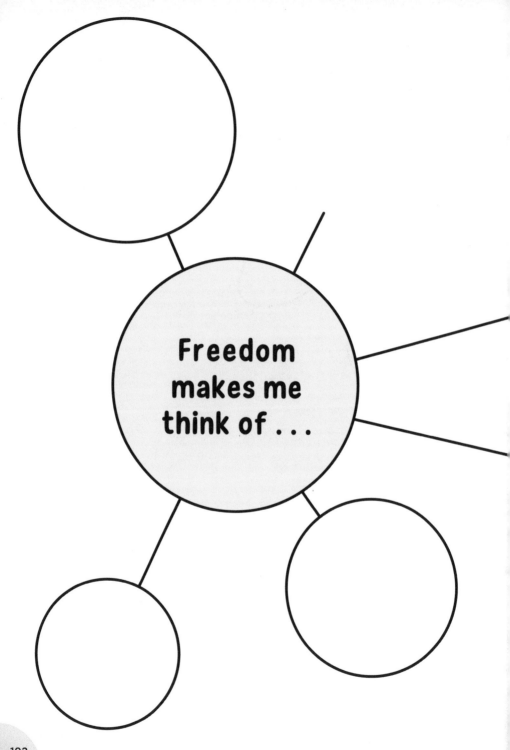

Freedom
makes me
think of . . .

All the feelings

I've felt today

Me riding a unicorn really fast

My flag

Battle Plan

We're stronger together.

Strategy Meeting

Protest

Dance Party

From: **To:**

Where: **When:**

From: **To:**

Where: **When:**

From: **To:**

Where: **When:**

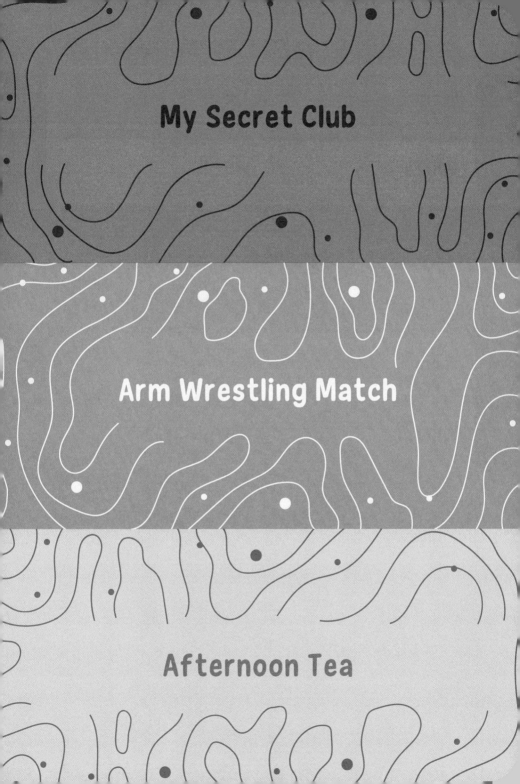

My Secret Club

Arm Wrestling Match

Afternoon Tea

From: **To:**

Where: **When:**

From: **To:**

Where: **When:**

From: **To:**

Where: **When:**

SPEAK.
THE WORLD
IS LISTENING.

Portrait of Me
by _____

What my future holds

Please stop giving me . . .

Thank you ALL!!!

One more thing . . .

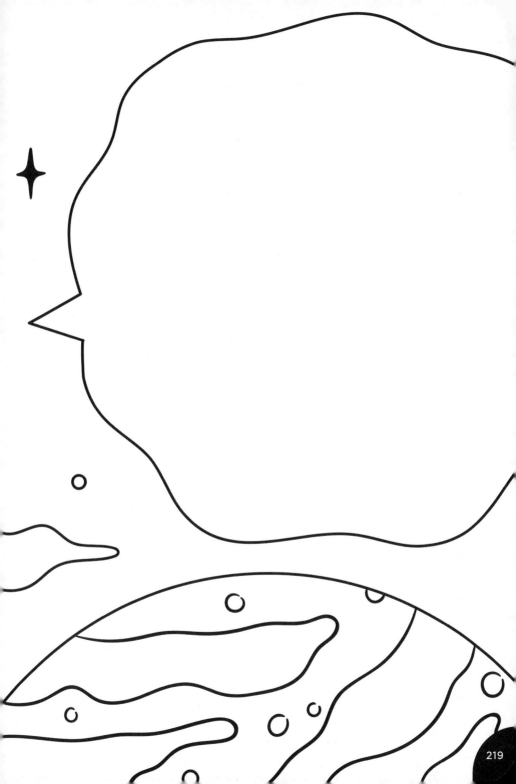

KEEP READING WITH REBEL GIRLS

www.rebelgirls.co

Good Night Stories for Rebel Girls

Good Night Stories for Rebel Girls 2

Good Night Stories for Rebel Girls Gift Box

GOOD NIGHT STORIES FOR REBEL GIRLS IS ALSO A BEAUTIFUL PODCAST!

Listen to the stories of incredible women read by some of the most influential voices of our time.

Go to **www.rebelgirls.co/podcast** or find it wherever you get your podcasts!

REVOLUTIONS
ARE FOR SHARING!

Join the Rebel Girls' community and share your creations
with fellow rebels all around the world.

Facebook: **www.facebook.com/rebelgirls**
Instagram: **@rebelgirlsbook**
Twitter: **@rebelgirlsbook**

Use the hashtags **#IAMAREBELGIRL** and **#REBELGIRLSJOURNAL**
in your posts and tell us about your journey as a rebel girl
on the Facebook group The Rebel Girls Movement:
facebook.com/groups/therebelmovement

We'll see you there!

★ Acknowledgments ★

Our heartfelt thank you goes to our unbelievable community of rebels, who once again supported our Kickstarter campaign with incredible enthusiasm and generosity. There is no better feeling than knowing we are not alone and that so many people out there are fighting for freedom and equality, each in their own way.

To our team, thank you for inspiring us every day. Thank you for your hard work, for your irony, for taking care of one another, and for never stepping back from a challenge. We could not be prouder of the company we're building together.

About the Authors

Francesca Cavallo and **Elena Favilli** are the *New York Times* best-selling authors and founders of the Rebel Girls movement. In 2016 and 2017, they broke records creating the most crowdfunded publishing campaigns in history to launch their book series Good Night Stories for Rebel Girls. In 2018, they won the *Publishers Weekly* Star Watch Award, produced their first podcast, and were nominated for a People's Choice Podcast Award. They grew up in Italy and live in Venice, California.

Timbuktu is an award-winning media company founded in 2012 by Elena Favilli (Chief Executive Officer) and Francesca Cavallo (Chief Creative Officer). Through a combination of thought-provoking content, stellar design, and business innovation, Timbuktu is redefining the boundaries of indie publishing to inspire a global community of progressive families spanning seventy countries. Timbuktu is home to a diverse and passionate group of rebels who work together in Los Angeles, New York, Atlanta, Mérida (Mexico), London, and Milan.

For occasional updates on our new projects, subscribe at: **www.rebelgirls.co/signup**

If you liked this book, please take a minute to review it!

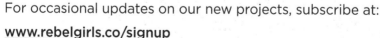